Kena

TERRA COTTA

pots with style

TERRA COTTA
pots with style

Anthony Noel

Special photography by Andrew Lawson

SOMA
san francisco

To Pam and Clem,
with love from Andy

First published in 1998 by Frances Lincoln. American Edition published 1998 by SOMA Books by arrangement with Frances Lincoln.

SOMA Books is an imprint   for SOMA Books:
of Bay Books & Tapes, Inc.   Publisher: James Connolly
For information, address: Art Director: Jeffrey O'Rourke
Bay Books & Tapes, Inc., 555 American Editor: Melinda Levine
De Haro Street, No. 220,   Proofreader: Marianna Cherry
San Francisco, CA 94107   Typesetting: Patrick David Barber

Library of Congress Cataloguing–in–Publication Data
Noel, Anthony. Terra cotta / Anthony Noel. --North American ed.
                    ISBN 1-57959-005-5   1. Container gardening.
            2. Terra-cotta. 3. Plant containers. I. Title. SB418.N64 1998
                                        717--dc21 97-46791 CIP

9 8 7 6 5 4 3 2 1   Printed in Hong Kong

ISBN 1-57959-005-5   Distributed to the trade by Publishers Group West

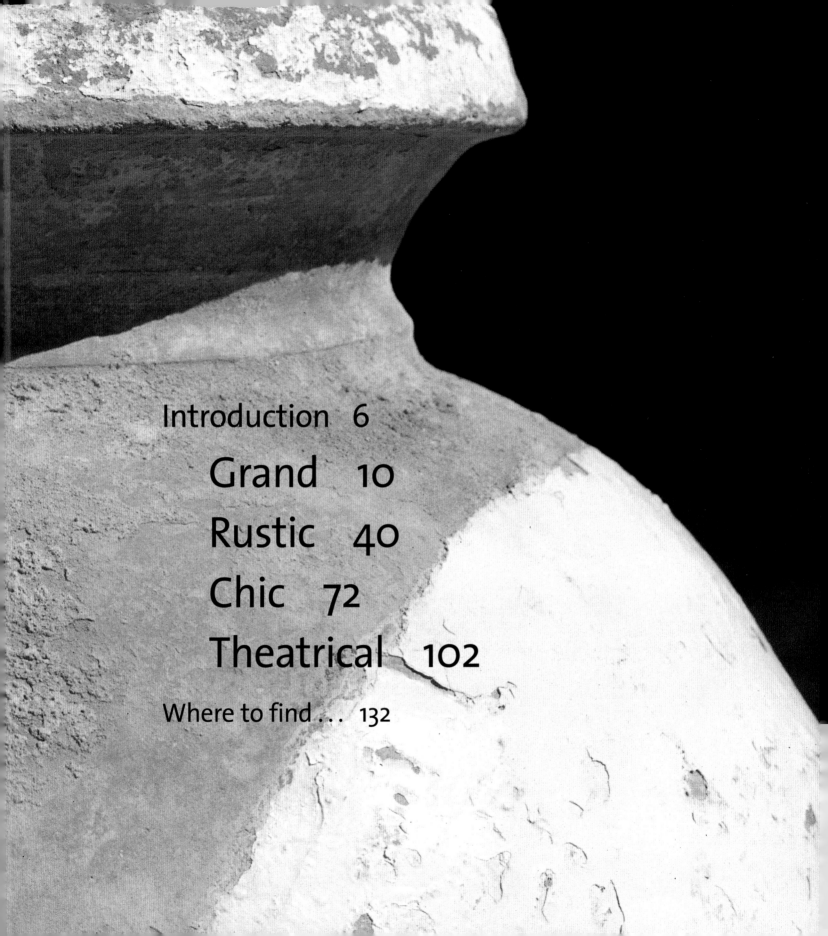

Introduction 6

Grand   10

Rustic   40

Chic   72

Theatrical   102

Where to find . . . 132

Introduction

From sunless city basement to vast ancestral acres (most of us live in places somewhere in between the two) there can hardly be a garden that wouldn't be improved by the addition of containers made from fired earth, or terra cotta. As natural as wood, stone, trees, water and flowers, no material could be more sympathetic or practical when fashioned into containers. It has to work — it is the very stuff from which all plant-life springs. However decoratively one uses terra cotta, it is impossible to remove its natural dignity, or make it pretentious — how could it be? Terra cotta is as old as civilization.

Terra cotta containers, planted with standard citrus trees and other foliage plants, bring natural warmth and grace to a small modern balcony.

You just can't get it wrong with terra cotta. It not only looks good, bringing warmth, naturalness and great decorative potential to any garden, but it is also perfect for the well-being of the plant. Terra cotta retains water, keeping the roots cool yet, being porous, it allows the plants to breathe.

Tall terra cotta pots are an imaginative choice of container for luscious red geraniums. Three in a row make a handsome display.

For me to attempt to write a history, or presume to explain the manufacturing of terra cotta, would be an impertinence. I could not do justice to this ancient and sophisticated art. Better to leave it to the experts! Instead, I feel it would be more helpful to show examples of the terra cotta that I admire, the ways I have tried to make it work for me and the way it could work for you. The most successful illustrations are a happy combination of handsome pot (however simple or ornate), good planting and the right position. It is all a question of style.

This elusive quality may be dictated by the terra cotta itself: its form, size and texture. The other approach is to impose your own style, by arrangement, location, planting or decoration. Style, therefore, has infinite variations, but for the purposes of this book, I describe four distinctive moods. In chapter 1, the mood is grand; in chapter 2, rustic; in chapter 3, chic; and, finally, in chapter 4, theatrical. I hope this will show you just how versatile terra cotta can be.

Anthony Noel.

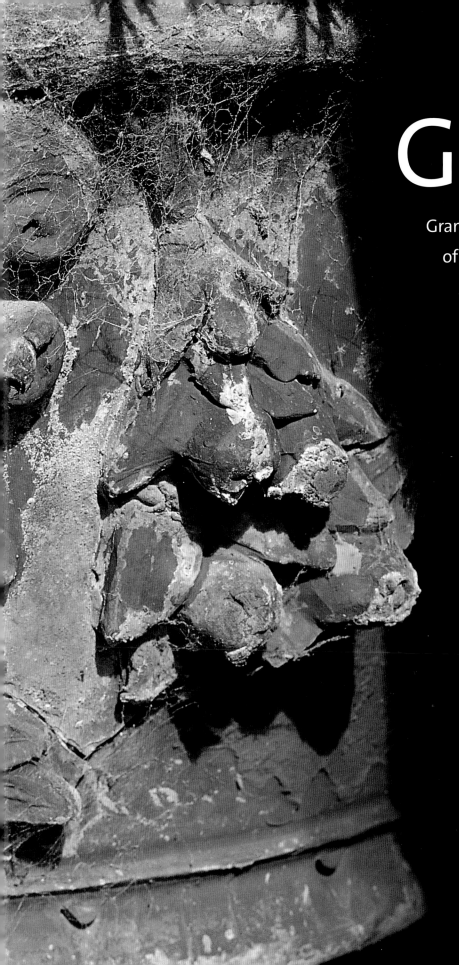

GRAND

Grand pots are the garden equivalent of diamonds. Always elegant, never vulgar and you cannot over-scale them. They are generous, abundant, not only lovely in themselves, but kind enough to make the plants they host look wonderful as well. True beauty that comes from sun-drenched earth has an innocence, too, and the more you look at these terra cotta pots, the more enchanting they become. Grandeur and simplicity in one. And, they grow old gracefully.

I remember the first time I saw Duchêne's dancing-water garden at Blenheim Palace in Oxford, England; I can't have been more than ten years old. I loved the contrast of the geometric beds and walkway against the background of the serpentine lake and hanging beechwoods. Equally exciting were the masses of blue agapanthus flowering in old, swagged terra cotta pots. The bright blue was magical against the water, and somehow the terra cotta, quite grand, lent just enough warmth to bring the whole composition to life.

I was fascinated by the huge pots that were almost as tall as I and couldn't resist touching one — it felt warm, unlike the cold stone. I ran my hand over the garland decorations, but it was swiftly pulled away so I would not do any damage. But the damage was already done. I begged my mother all the way home to buy some pots like those so we could have them in our garden.

That child is still very much alive in me today. I can see no reason why such majesty cannot be brought into all our gardens, particularly now when there is so much more decorative

This is exactly the sort of grandeur that inspired me as a child: a massive pot with lid, smooth and round, covered with a kind of decorative detail — simply etched moldings, flowing handles and formal medallion beneath the maker's name — that begs to be touched. The matching lid with its pretty, urn-shaped finial, makes this a rare piece: a restrained, elegant design, weathered slightly over time.

Terra cotta doesn't come much more ornate than this; close up, it is incredible (see page 10). Yet, here, it is comfortable in a corner of a small-town garden. One of the beauties of terra cotta is its ability to lend style and warmth to any exterior (or interior) space — regardless of how small. In a confined location, a decorated pot steals, rather than demands, attention; surrounding objects will share its glory.

The grandeur of this piece calls for simple, bold planting. When the marguerites become tired toward the end of summer, they will be replaced with white lace-cap hydrangeas; then black-and-white pansies, or white lily-flowered tulips will follow in spring.

terra cotta readily available and at affordable prices. You don't have to be a duke, these days, to enjoy the grandeur of a baroque palace; nor do you have to possess vast riches to re–create a villa garden in your own backyard.

Scale it up

Talking of your own backyard, why not indeed? For, however large these pots, most of them will travel home in the back of a car. Take a risk with size — you will be surprised at what you can get away with.

I learned a valuable lesson in scale several years ago when I temporarily placed a large terra cotta swagged pot in my living room, complete with palm tree. Its twin was delayed in Italy for some reason and one would have looked unbalanced outside where I had originally planned to place the pair: one on each side of a garden step. So indoors the pot went. A friend who came to supper that night could not get over it, and said how wonderfully bold I had been, what style and so on. The truth is, the pot did look imposing in the room, and yet outside, where the sky is the ceiling, its proportions were just right.

Planting for effect

Now the fun begins. Let your imagination run away with you, but be daring! Mop-headed boxwood trees look terrific in these decorative pots and will grow in shade, as will the taller bay trees. So will yews, up to a point, but these look better trimmed into cones, possibly in a larger space. Try busy-lizzies (the double ones are most attractive, if you can find them), tobacco plants or strawflower around your boxwood.

In smaller swagged pots, you could try hostas (which will also perform in shade), particularly the blue- or gray-leaved *Hosta sieboldiana* 'Elegans'. If you have some that have been eaten alive by slugs and snails, transplant them at any time of the year, put a ring of vaseline around the top of the container, keep the plants well watered and after a while you will have something stunning. In the sun, of course, life is much easier. I'm fond of petunias and the pretty way they tumble over the edge of the pot, particularly the white, and striped varieties—the deep violet ones smell delicious and look great planted with heliotrope.

This is a magnificent old terra cotta pot. Coming upon it suddenly at Kiftsgate Court, Gloucester, England, (home of the famous white rose 'Kiftsgate'), I was stopped in my tracks. As a rule, I prefer containers to be more simply planted than this, but where you want to introduce notes of splendor, you can't go wrong with bold plants in a layered planting. Why should the grand places have all the fun? This feast of flowers would look equally magnificent in the smallest backyard. Here, we have the rare honey-bush (*Melianthus major*) with its gray serrated leaves, both the variegated red (which sparkles) and the candy pink, ivy-leaved geraniums, and an assortment of fuchsias and strawflowers. The dignified old pot loves it all.

Italian inspiration . . .

Italian terra cotta pots planted with lemon trees give ornamental structure to one of the most romantic of the Tuscan pleasure gardens, the Boboli Gardens at the Pitti Palace, situated within the walls of Florence. Andromeda on her rock is the focus of the water garden. It might be difficult to re-create statuary, balustrades and water on this scale, but terra cotta, like fine furniture, will add distinction anywhere.

Faced with a space of say, 15 x 20 feet, make a short gravel walk, positioning Boboli-style pots on each side, and terminate it with a sunken pool, or even a larger pot elevated on flagstone.

If your garden is no more than a sunless lightwell, set one of these Italian terra cotta beauties in the center and plant it with a pyramid of shade-tolerant yew or ivy trained on canes. Try adding a row of smaller pots all around the edge. Keep it formal and architectural — that's the secret!

. . . and realization

Here is the garden of my old home. I loved this place. A city garden, only 15 x 39 feet, but the terra cotta pots have far higher aspirations.

Always aware that there are lessons to be learned from the great gardens of the past, I made it my business to visit as many of them as possible before designing my garden. On one such visit, I saw swagged pots used in a modest courtyard and it fired my imagination. When my friends suggested giving me a pot for the garden, I was delighted. Although it seemed enormous in the store, once I got it home, it looked so great I promptly went out and ordered three more. Planted with mop-headed boxwood and poor man's orchids (*Schizanthus pinnatus*), the large pieces transformed my ordinary brick-paved yard.

Paradise transported

It is these scenes in life that make us long to garden, to create our own corner of paradise.

◄ The Isola Bella in Lombardy, northern Italy, was built by architect Angelo Crivelli to look like a treasure-seeking galleon. A statue of Vulcan stands on the deck, while cannon balls of green boxwood in simple terra cotta pots lead the way down to the water theater. This built-up site is a difficult one in practical terms; nevertheless the dream was there, and it was made to come true.

▶ Put your hand over the black-and-white clapboard cottage at the top of this picture and find yourself suddenly transported to a corner of a classical Italian garden. All the ingredients are there: a wonderful, antiquated terra cotta pot, lemon-scented star jasmine clipped into a sphere, and the rich foliage of a low boxwood hedge.

Grand

▲ Giovanni Vanni, 1841, terra cotta artist, etched in Roman letters and signed with an embossed flower. Magic! This grand pot is all the more appealing for having been repaired; the color of its pitted surface lies somewhere between burnt caramel and the soft red of old marble.

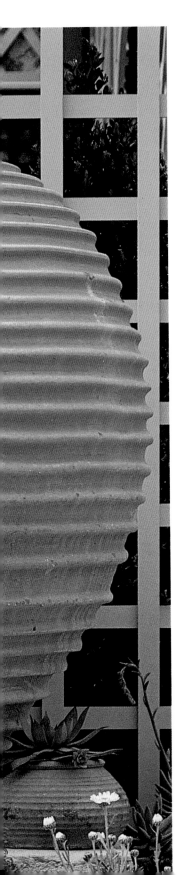

Simple stature

These three pots impress with their magnitude, needing little in the way of backdrop or planting to make them grand. They share similar proportions, but the variation in their texture, color and age creates different effects.

◄As modern as tomorrow, this huge ribbed globe reminds me of those Sputnik-inspired lamps of the late 1950s. It just needs three metal legs — narrow-based amphoras are often designed to rest on iron frameworks. This pot is flanked by miniature versions that make the scale seem overblown. Pots this large make better solitary features and, with the possible exception of milkweed (*Euphorbia wulfenii*), I would resist the temptation to plant this one with anything. Let simple stature speak for itself.

▲ The superb quality of this modern glazed pot, blue as the Mediterranean, makes it very grand. It could be planted with a gray-leaved palm, or agave but, like the pots opposite, it is impressive left empty. Don't be put off by the color wash — containers this good only enhance their surroundings.

Palatial texture

Would you call the pyramids plain, if they stood next to the Taj Mahal? Grandeur is about size and shape, relative to setting.

Grand terra cotta can take many forms. Here are two very different pieces: one shiny, sophisticated and classical; the other massive, uncompromising and weathered. Both would be at home in a palace, and both will make a backyard palatial.

The black basalt glaze and intricate molding of the urn is immediately decorative, but it is no more impressive than the plainer majesty of the white amphora. The urn is given resonance by a formal lawn and statuary; the amphora presides over a planting of challenging forms and textures: spiky New Zealand flax and a spreading Japanese maple.

High society

As a general rule, the higher a container can be placed, the more commanding it will look.

◀◀ This elegant pedestal and urn rises out of the undergrowth — a lonely vertical that draws the eye upward, giving focus to the overhanging foliage. Romantically, it seems to evoke the sunroom of a a ruined 19th-century estate, reinforced by the lovely camellia in full flower (a greenhouse favorite), and the ivy that drips from the urn like the forgotten progeny of some long-ago houseplant.

◀ The character of this beautiful urn could not be more different: faded terra cotta, fashioned into a wide, shallow bowl on a stone base. The effect of this arrangement is less formal than that of the container on the far left. The different pots and objects seem to be chatting together in the shade, while the rest of the world takes a siesta.

Singular sensations

Take advantage of outdoor architectural elements: balustrades, walls, and staircases are perfect for punctuation.

▶ This lovely view reminds me of the first time I saw Florence. It was early spring and every courtyard and balcony seemed to boast pots of deciduous azaleas in flower, some of them very large indeed. Placed securely on the parapet of an ancient staircase, these azaleas in putty-colored pots light up the old stone. Their presence between every flight of stairs enhances the rhythm of the architecture.

◀ Like a finial at the foot of a grand staircase, this generous pot makes an excellent full stop, the color of the fuchsias echoed in the walls. Confident and stylish, this is a planting and a position that takes the spotlight.

▶ This exquisitely planted basket of twinspur (*Diascia barberae*), fuchsia and lobelia resembles a soufflé of raspberries and cream. The lightness of the concoction feels right against a background of dark green yew. On a base of lichened stone, the terra cotta marks the head of the staircase, leading you toward it. At the foot of the stairs, its delicacy might have been overwhelmed.

Decorative detail

Small spaces don't have to stick to humble ideas, they can accommodate grand objets d'art that exude atmosphere, without being overpowering. You only have to look at some of the smaller enclosures of the great gardens open to the public, to see that this is true.

There are three aspects to bear in mind. 1) Proportion: the picture should fit the frame, in this case, the trellis that comfortably surrounds the swagged pot and statue. 2) Planting: this should form a natural setting for the objects, suggesting everything has been there for a long time. 3) Understatement: don't overdo it; understate the colors, and choose two features, not a dozen. This bronze figure has a natural quietness. The same is true of the decorated terra cotta pot (which will look even better as rain water stains it with a patina of lime, encouraging moss and lichens). Boxwood is a good choice for the terra cotta container (see pages 22–23); to substitute gaudy annuals would ruin this charming scene.

Center point

This story is all about contrast — smooth, round pots and towering angular plants that stand out wherever you choose to put them.

▶ Water and architectural planting, like architecture and music, go well together. This is a splendid choice for a container planting, a striped cordyline in a modern amphora is really eye-catching. When seen as a reflection in the sunken pool, its impact will be doubled, but the natural illusion won't overpower the little garden. Curly-leaved hostas at the foot of the pot contrast with the cordyline, but subtly echo the shape of the container — their color is an additional complement. An excellent focal point showing taste (often a rare commodity in modern gardening), wit and imagination.

▶▶ By clever planting and positioning, this container has been turned into something that could grace the grandest mansion of the biggest film star in Beverly Hills. The background is dark and luxurious, but this leaves center stage free for the true star to perform. Placed on an island in a sea of gravel, all eyes focus on the wide-mouthed terra cotta container and its swishing, rustling palm. Even the humble nasturtiums at the foot of the amphora play their part.

▶▶▶ The entrance to this town house is made so much more impressive by the grand pot and its flourish of New Zealand flax, pointing the way to the front door. Spiky leaves and gentle terra cotta balance each other perfectly.

Focal fireworks

In some ways, these pots are opposites: one features a spectacular plant; the other is almost buried beneath a mass of tiny flowers. The thought behind both is the same: position and planting to stop you in your tracks.

◄Doesn't this old pot look great? Glimpsed through a gap in the hedge, the delicate pink fireworks of *Lavatera thuringiaca* 'Barnsley', twinspur (*Diascia barberae*) and geraniums make it a focal point par excellence. Quirky planting and its position on an old millstone restrain any excess of grandeur.

▶Imagine coming upon this high fashion statement in the middle of a woodland walk. What fun! Fifth Avenue in the depths of the garden. The verdigris glazed pot makes a gorgeous container for a mouthful of tumbling flowers in pale pink. It works

because blue is present in all four colours of the planting—including the verbena leaves. The sizzling pot is not set apart from the background, but it is still a focal point of grandiose character. It gives scale to the trees, enhancing their elegant limbs, and its bold colors break up the emerald carpet of ground cover.

Contained exuberance

Choice plants and a little imagination will turn the humblest terra cotta container into a spectacular showpiece.

▶ This garden has the kind of grand garden structure that, most of us, with our limited resources, can only aspire to have: a beautifully laid path of old brick, a raised pool with dolphin fountain and impressive curving pedestals. Yet, the most exciting feature is a plain terra cotta container, exploding with flowers — alyogyne, felicia, lobelia, verbena. In a terra cotta pot, exuberant planting is always within the realms of possibility.

▶▶ What an incredible planting! With nothing more than a second-hand chimney pot and a collection of plants available from any flower stand, an artist (and artist, he or she surely is) has created a fountain of sophisticated color. The cordyline waves high in the air; felicia, red and white fuchsia, variegated strawflower, lavender and verbena all dance together, while the delicate, ivy-leaved geranium overflows onto the floor. Who says chimney pots can't be grand?

RUSTIC

The country. Sweet air, wholesome food
and time to spare . . . but you do not
need to pack up and leave the city. The
garden can be the perfect canvas for
rustic style and there is no better
means than terra cotta to provide it.
The simplest pots, unglazed, weathered
or worn, will bring pastoral bliss to the
smallest urban space.

We, all of us, need to get back to our roots. The grandest lady of her time, Marie Antoinette, with the luxury and decadence of Versailles at her fingertips, strangely enough, wanted nothing more than to play the shepherdess. *La vie rustique* was her escape. She even built an artificial mill.

Today, we too seek to recreate this simple style; it represents a complete contrast to the fast, busy lives we lead. Think of the pine-scrubbed chairs and tables piled high in urban showrooms! Or the fashion for kitchen gardens with wire fruit baskets, rows of lettuces and spring carrots, the newest, tiniest potatoes.

In our rustic idyll, we picture glass plant covers, neatly stacked against cold frames, and, by a bed of rhubarb, five or six old terra cotta force pots, of different shapes and sizes, which stand casually around on the cinder path — like actors waiting for a call to the stage. Some are repaired, some lichened and lime stained, others mossy, but they all miraculously retain their tops. In colors ranging from buff to ocher, soft orange to black-red — each one is evocative of rural charm.

I love old vegetable pots. Here, three sea kale pots and a rhubarb force pot offer their gentle textures to delight us. These charming, easygoing old-timers have been placed as if they, too, are growing among the herbs.

One of the advantages of terra cotta is that it is so easy to move around, unlike heavy stone. The different effects that can be created are endless. These well-used vegetable pots have this potential. They are, of course, working containers, traditionally found in the kitchen garden, but they are decorative pieces in their own right. You get the feeling that they would be equally happy living on a balcony in town, turned upside-down with their tops inside, making a home for some treasured plant.

A working life

The essence of rustic style — for style it has become — is that the terra cotta served a purpose. Rhubarb force pots have their own function, but turned upside down with the lids used as bases, they make terrific planters. Leave them unadorned, planted with a standard gooseberry, red currant or gnarled vine and maybe bordered with chives or emerald parsley. Consider recycling old chimney pots (if you can find whimsical ones with feet, their silhouettes can be enchanting) and planting them with cottage flowers. Or try the antique wine or olive oil jars now beginning to trickle out of Spain. They look great, these amphoras, but they can be overpowering and have to be used sparingly, where they won't dominate a garden setting. I like to see them upside down, where their satisfying shape reminds me of the dome of a chapel, on a remote Greek island . . .

Early morning, midsummer, in an idyllic country kitchen garden. The terra cotta rhubarb force pots have completed their task for the year — until next spring only their decorative presence is required in the garden.

Cottage planting

Planting, too, will help you capture rustic style. Sunflowers, wild strawberries, ornamental cabbages. Larkspurs, sweet williams, love-in-a-mist, pinks, violas, pansies. Tiny spring bulbs, scented-leaved geraniums, morning glories, *Cobaea scandens*, sweet peas, lavenders and nasturtiums. All look well and do well in pots. If you can find old pots, they will look even better.

Pots of herbs placed near the kitchen door, or on the windowsill are pretty and useful and they will appreciate the drainage the terra cotta provides. Outside the back door, I have a pot containing only parsley — as rich a color as any flower and marvellous juxtaposed with white.

Tricks of the trade

Simple decoration and style tricks enhance the rustic ambience. You could add checks to the odd pot (like gingham curtains in a cottage window); or for extra sparkle, you could whitewash it (this looks great as it peels off). Add a wood basket, an antiquated wheelbarrow overflowing with geraniums; look for old garden tools, a watering can or rusty hoe to complete the country pose.

Rustic

46

Now here is something after my own heart — I love these old pots and would never want to be without them in any garden, anywhere. Stacked in a corner with nothing in them, their weathered finishes look great, bringing to the garden the same venerable quality as old brick walls or ancient flagstones. Being hand-thrown, each one is slightly different in texture, color and shape — charming in its own right. Pots like these mellow as old wine does, their character improving with each chip, lime stain, or bloom of moss or lichen. It is these little imperfections that give them personality.

Even better to pile up pots in a forgotten barrow, and fill them with a profusion of white, shocking pink and red geraniums. Simple cottage-style planting will bring rustic style to the tiniest urban garden.

Oil jars & olive groves

What a perfect place for a picnic — a solitary visit to be alone with your thoughts, or a clandestine meeting with a lover under the stars. This venerable amphora, unadorned and unrefined, creates a peaceful space around it. Placed without pretension on a stone base, it looks wonderful under the old olive tree — enhancing the view, but not too much.

You could plant something simple in this pot without overembellishing the scene, perhaps single, blush-colored geraniums, nasturtiums or morning glories. Spotlights hidden in the tree would throw the pot into dramatic shadow; or keep the mood mellow with natural dappled light.

Up the garden path

Let the large kitchen gardens of country houses inspire you to recreate the mood on a snippet of a site.

Not many of us have the room these days for a full-blown kitchen garden of winding brick paths, flower-cutting borders and sprawling rows of vegetables. Yet, even in the smallest space, there is no reason why we can't borrow some of the delightful paraphernalia and enjoy its reassuring charm. On the right, an old rhubarb force pot has found its way into a more urban scene. With a boxwood spiral in cheeky juxtaposition, the planting is a jumble of semiwild viburnum and cottage-garden favorites — feverfew, hydrangea, ornamental onion, regal lilies, and towering sea holly (*Eryngium gigantuem*). This makes for a charming countrified scene. Sweet peas, runner beans, even the odd lettuce or tomato plant, could be added later.

▲ The flowers of the lovely cape cowslip (*Lachenalia*) remind me of old-fashioned English barley-sugar candy. Even in the most picturesque setting, I think it deserves the distinction of a weathered container (make sure you plant it no less than 3 inches deep or the bulbs will split). Here, the texture of this lime-encrusted pot emphasizes its delicacy.

The cape cowslip enjoys a baking in summer but it likes to be well watered. It is worth taking a little trouble with this pretty creature — if the amber-colored flowers aren't enough, look at those tiger markings on the leaf and stem!

The patina of time

Weathered textures are the key to rustic pots. Their roughness is the ideal counterpart to a planting, or a background of delicate color.

▶ With imagination, this container resembles a toppled sweet jar — its contents scattered all over the floor. Originally, it saw a working life containing one family's olive oil or wine supply. Hundreds of years old, its marvelous texture has evolved under the elements and, since it is made of the same stuff from which the plants grow, it is perfectly at home now in the sun, among the profusion of flowers. Its crumbling exterior enhances their vitality. In this situation, the oil jar has the quality of a cornucopia, or horn of plenty — it seems to offer sustenance to the plants, as it once did to people.

The gentle touch

Hand-crafted pots have a special charm. Thrown on a wheel, or pressed into a mold by hand, each pot is different — it's up to you how you use it.

◀ You can never have too many miniature pots. They are perfect for nestling in odd nooks and crannies, planted and playing host to bunches of flowers. This one is lovely for its narrow rim and crumbly texture, resembling the crust of a Camembert cheese, a speckled pear, or a warm red Italian peach. I have repainted my own collection many times and, after a few years outside, the paint peels off and you regain that charming texture.

▶ These large rustic pots are increasingly rare, but it is still possible to find them at country markets and antique shops. They have the same diversity of color and shape as their smaller cousins and, more often than not, they are lightly decorated. Those are drainage holes drilled on the side, a sure way to recognize a handmade pot.

Unearthed treasure

Scavenging in stores can unearth the prettiest terra cotta gems. Hunt in junk shops, garden centers and markets to amass a collection of interesting pieces.

◄ The smallest backyard in the world has room for a slate shelf and a tiny arrangement of rustic pottery – you don't need sunshine! Take a couple of ordinary brackets, some used slate or stained wood, and a drill. Apply some pretty stone paint and introduce a couple of decorative climbers, such as honeysuckle vines. It doesn't matter if your terra cotta treasures are chipped and repaired — it adds to the charm. Look for variation in texture and shape — a smooth pot beside a rough-hewn jar — or anything with handles or a floral decoration. I like to keep a little terra cotta collection, to change when the mood strikes me.

▲ This beautifully textured container is hard to resist for an inner-city rustic collection. Look out for square, shallow bulb troughs, deep old saucers, multiholed strawberry planters, tiny thimble-sized jars, even fragments of grand pots. With a little confidence, you will be surprised what you can do.

Ways to display

Once you have acquired some rustic terra cotta, it is fun to take the look further with the addition of a few props.

Rustic

▼ Old galvanized florist's buckets and watering cans can be purchased inexpensively, likewise gardening baskets

and handmade tools. I have an old wood rake that I place nonchalantly in a corner — it looks great — a witch's broom would be equally effective. Under cover, neatly stacked wood seed boxes make a charming backdrop, and a great bunch of raffia hanging on a nail is decorative and useful.

▶ A simple shelf unit with pretty overhanging eaves becomes a miniature theater. This is a wonderful, modest way of displaying those plates, pots and tops that are too small in scale for the garden; decorate with honeysuckle and climbing hydrangea; add some chalky blue paint here and there. To my mind, this recalls the auricula theaters of the 18th and 19th centuries, built by country people to show off their wonderful plants.

The terra cotta need not be very expensive. This is a collection of old favorites, bits and pieces, lost and found. One could even plant them with auricula primroses, in which case paint the shelves matte black, for a burst of color in springtime.

Simply put

One simple vessel — an amphora, a basket — positioned with care, is often all the decoration an outdoor space requires.

◀◀A doorway makes a frame for a small amphora, placed to one side; this, with the plants clustering at ground level, serves to set the pot in context — it is not lost in space. There is a sense of enclosure, the arbor draped in bougainvillea softening the sky. The old pitted retaining walls are a decoration in themselves, perfectly in harmony with this rustic ornament.

◀When the surroundings are strong, it can be inappropriate to make a great big statement. With this beautiful curved-tile roof as backdrop, any pot or ornament is going to be upstaged. Much better gracefully to admit defeat and make a simple gesture to enhance the roof. In this instance, a terra cotta basket overflowing with flowers has a pretty plaited handle to adjust the focus. Casually placed, it improves the old stone parapet, without challenging the view behind.

Bashful heroes

Rustic terra cotta is gentle by nature. It may need some assistance in drawing attention to itself. Capture it with a window frame, or leave plenty of space around it.

◀ How comfortable this old handmade pot looks, peeking out of the cottage window. Set off perfectly by the lead window panes, a well-grown zonal geranium helps bring it to our attention, its pretty variegated leaves picking up the color of the old stone walls.

These geraniums are as easy to look after as a fireside cat; all they ask is a place in the sun (and shelter indoors from frost), regular watering and deadheading, and an occasional dinner of liquid tomato food. To propagate them is simplicity itself: in the spring, break off the new shoots with four or five leaves and firmly push them into sandy soil around the edge of a clay pot, about 1 inch apart. Water sparingly. In six weeks, you will have plants enough for an army of pots.

▶ The test of a garden is how it looks in winter, everything pared down to bare essentials — you can really see the bones of a place. Fired earth looks great in the cold; this terra cotta force pot has warmth of its own, a comforting landmark in a frozen environment.

Frost-proof terra cotta (check with your supplier) stands up well to freezing temperatures; its main enemy is a thorough soaking just before a heavy frost. So, if you find yourself watering a potted plant during the winter, do it in the morning, even if cold weather isn't forecast.

Softening the edges

Planting in rustic pots can be simple cottage style, or more eccentric for charming effect. These are flamboyant flowers in humble containers, the sort of thing you might notice driving through villages in the South of France.

▶ Jostling for space on a stone base, the informality of this quartet of pots is unexpected, especially with the unusual planting: echeveria on the left, navelwort (*Omphalodes luciliae*) on the right, a splash of red from a miniature rose, and the exotic shrub *Dunalia* (syn. *Acnistus*) *australis*, grown as a climber, against the house wall.

▶▶ Bold spires of summer hyacinth (*Galtonia candicans*) are a surprise here. Its subtle colors and irregular shape under-play the dramatic plant, anchoring it to earth. Closer to the ground, velvety petunias extend the texture of their pots and soften the edges of the stone steps. This arrangement draws attention to the doorway, and mitigates the severity of the architecture.

▼ Here we have a quieter theme. Van Gogh might have appreciated these old pots of sunflowers and French or Spanish lavender (*Lavandula stoechas*). Position bowls wherever you want the evocative scent to linger. Bold sunflowers (*Helianthus annuus*) make the perfect companions in treasured pots.

▶ Rosemary, sage, tarragon and a sprig of ivy. These rhubarb forcers capture the spirit of traditional cottage gardening — vegetables and herbs to sustain the family grow alongside seeds, cuttings from friends, and the occasional surprise from the neighbor's garden.

▶ This terra cotta bird surveying a dish of fleabane (*Erigeron*) and nemesia makes me smile. Together with the garden planting, this little scene has the innocence and freshness of a June morning in the country.

◀ Cistus, pinks and lavender cotton (*Santolina chamaecyparissus*) — all of the whimsical, scented flowers that we remember from our childhood — surround a funny old pot that's always been there. Actually, the pot is a fine antique of unusual shape. It would probably fetch quite a lot of money today.

By the end of the season, the nemesia and strawflower will have hidden the pot completely.

▶▶ Petunia, osteospermum, verbena, and *Tanacetum parthenium* — this is another group of old favorites. Planted in a delightfully jumbled fashion, this is a cottage garden in miniature. Its charm lies in the bright gravel setting, the contrasting pinks of the flowers and the texture of the pot. It looks as if it has been scrubbed, then left to dry in the sun — for a hundred years.

Urban retreat

Terra cotta transports the tranquility of a country hideaway to a high-rise terrace in the heart of the city.

◀ I take my hat off to the owner of this little balcony. High above the city's roar, growing anything at all is a daunting prospect. These two pots are a wonderful sight against the sky-scrapers, their simplicity perfectly complemented by a colorful winter planting of white chrysanthemums, ornamental cabbages and pansies. Brave little faces bring a breath of country air to a scene that could not be more urban.

▶ Simply planted pots of country edibles: wild strawberry, parsley, the welcome foliage of hosta, and handsome robust chairs, create a pastoral scene beneath a well-made trellis. When the roses and wisteria have had a chance to grow, this will be an even more magical place.

CHIC

Jackie Kennedy, Princess Grace, Marlene Dietrich. Chanel, Schiaparelli, Dior. Chocolate-and-cream Pullman cars, the color white. London, Paris, New York.

Chic people. Chic ideas. Chic gardens.

Chic is deliberate, smart and understated. Stylish, elegant and urbane, it says expensive. Strange, you might think, for a terra cotta flower pot, yet terra cotta can be amazingly chic. It is simply a question of pot, planting, style — get these in the right combination and, with terra cotta, chic is yours.

A deliberate art

Chic containers are sleek and sculpted. Understated, subtle, there is secrecy in their control and a deliberateness about their pose. They hint at the past, but enhance the present. A collection of amphoras evoke the kasbah in Marrakech, but positioned at the entrance to a sophisticated town house, they make a fashionable statement. Be worldly wise with ethnic terra cotta — use it to transcend the boundaries of time and space.

The silver-and-white garden at Sissinghurst in Kent, England is supremely chic because, though dramatic, it is also restrained. Under its central canopy of white *Rosa mulliganii* lives an old Ali Baba pot from Morocco. Seen through a wrought-iron gate is another ancient pot, this time larger, planted with *Astelia nervosa* 'Silver Spear'. These are ethnic pots in a surprising location: with their sophisticated planting, they are the essence of chic.

The elegant orchid, lily, amaryllis and bird-of-paradise demand plain, preferably old, pots. To plant them in containers as elaborate as the flowers would ruin the look.

A trio of oil jars makes a powerful statement. The pots have elegance and poise, sharing similar features — proud, raised shoulders and drawn-in chests — significantly, however, they are not the same. The spirit of rebellion is manifest in their asymmetry; they cast a cool, oblique stare from one side of the steps.

Bold with brushes

Sometimes, a little embellishment is chic. When I first opened my garden to the public, it should have been dressed to kill, but I felt it lacked a certain zest. The planting was gray, green and white — it needed definition. I knew black-and-white awnings would have been the answer, but it was too late. The only solution was to take a chance and stripe the flower pots. I loved the results and have been painting pots ever since. You can enhance the natural color of terra cotta with a range of glazes, or transform pots completely with a color wash.

Indoors, painted pots can echo the color scheme of the rooms of the house. For an elegant gray-blue and white dining room, I painted three large, modern pots to use instead of a windowbox. The sill was wide and incorporated handsome wrought-iron acanthus leaves. I mixed stone paint to match one of the blues in the room, leaving the rims of the pots exposed. In each pot I planted a large boxwood ball. Privacy, style and low maintenance in one! With these, little further decoration was necessary.

Black and white is the essence of chic — expensive, tailored and restrained — with a dash of panache. This smart scene is a study in sophisticated textures. White on white and black on black. The graceful white agapanthus flowers echo the shiny, white, painted terra cotta containers, while the glossy black of the trellis in the background is picked up by black patent wrapping paper underneath.

In this urban setting, the elegant agapanthus foliage is hardly countrified. The lion, like a sculpture on the park gates, looks on indifferently — he has seen it all before. Refreshing as *la vie rustique* can be, it's good to be back in town.

This Spanish interior, with its black-and-white checked marble floor and slender classical columns, is an essay in the art of symmetrical styling — without trying too hard. Palms and ferns in formal terra cotta containers, positioned deliberately, like pieces on a chessboard, balance the lanterns and chairs on each side of the central door. The restrained architecture dictates the way the room is decorated. Cool black, white and soft lime are relieved by the green plants and warm terra cotta pots.

Fashionable flowers

The classic color scheme for painted pots is black (or the darkest green) and white. Either of these looks marvelous with soft lime, soft gray, the worn-out turquoise of old French chairs, putty green and dusty pink stripes. In black or white pots, why not try some black flowers: 'Molly Sanderson' and 'Bowles' Black' violets, widow iris, *Ophiopogon planiscapus* 'Nigrescens', 'Lord Bute' geranium, black fritillary and black parrot tulips.

Outdoors indoors

Chic terra cotta bridges the gap between indoors and out. I have even seen a fully grown *Rhododendron* 'Fragrantissimum' moved into the deep window recess of a castle library.

For a lunch or dinner party setting, contrast small box mop-headed or ball boxwood in old flower pots with exquisite china.

Other indoor planting can include exotic palms and ferns, delphinium, hellebore, narcissus, snowdrops, or pyramids of gently forced winter jasmine or grape hyacinth.

Flagrant display

There is inspiration to be found in nearly all the gardens of the world, even if what moves us is simply a planting combination, or a particular way of placing a pot.

▶ Terra cotta in the New York Botanical Gardens brings glamor to the municipal garden. The length of the pool is dotted with potted palms on pedestals. It looks great — warm terra cotta, overflowing with exotic foliage on crisp white. It might not always be possible to dazzle on this scale, but you can use the same principle on a balcony, terrace or path at home. Even a tiny terra cotta pot can turn heads when placed on a table-top as a decorative centerpiece.

▶▶ The calamondin mimics the spread of its larger relations; you could create a series of wooden platforms, placing on each one a tiny tree in a terra cotta pot.

Just dessert

Molded terra cotta has the sensuous grace of sculpted candy — sugar icing and molasses–colored tones, the delicious textures of the confectioner's art . . .

◀ This terra cotta bottle has the smooth texture and color of a pink sugared almond. It would be enchanting surrounded by low, gray-leaved plants such as 'Mrs. Sinkins' carnation, campion (*Silene maritima*) and thyme (*Thymus neiceffi*), its reflection captured in a small formal pool. In the background, I imagine white lavender, pink, cream and green variegated jasmine scrambling about and, for height, perhaps a white-flowered verbascum such as 'Mont Blanc'. Or, the jar could even be placed beside the bath, filled with attar of rose or pink champagne.

▶ For decorative effect, I would leave these pink and caramel-colored terra cotta hearts at the bottom of a bowl of water, then float white or cream-toned roses on the surface. Placed on a low table or wide step, you could look into the water and glimpse the delicious terra cotta shapes swirling about.

Self-containers

Terra cotta in elegant shapes graces the garden with its presence. Choose pastel pinks and smoky shades for the last word in exterior chic.

◄The charm of this fascinating giant lies in its subtleties: the horizontally etched lines, the piecrust molding, the deeper carvings around the top and the gentle, curving shape. I would love to move this to a more prominent location, but judging by the girth of the fig tree's trunk, I think it is firmly ensconced where it is! *Ficus carica* is ideal in a container: restricted roots encourage it to produce fruit.

▶ An unglazed, biscuit-colored container and a finial, drizzled with chartreuse, look as if they originate from a chic

delicatessen near La Madeleine in Paris. It is perfect unplanted, but how charming a row would look, teeming with marguerites in summer. Alternatively, you could reinforce the shape of the pretty finial with a miniature boxwood spiral and plant the pot with the green rose, *Rosa* x *odorata* 'Viridiflora', with its curious peppery scent.

◄The flowing lines and texture of this modern pot remind me of sculpted leather boots, or a snappy clutch bag from a stylish boutique. It demands a plain setting: a bed of dark green ivy; low mounds of clipped boxwood; or perhaps large, mossy cobblestones.

Tailored grace

The great couturiers, always able to pull a show stopper out of the bag, are also capable of making a perfectly cut little black dress. This is what chic is all about — understatement with flair.

▲▲ These miniature striped long pots are excellent examples of subtle decoration, giving rhythm to the terra cotta. The horizontal stripes make a stable visual base for the agave, strong enough to stand up to the old wall, whereas the delicate palm demands the elegance of vertical lines. The soft, natural, terra cotta pinks enhance the rich color of the old stone.

▶ Light, elegant and unexpected, these slender pots are so chic — they look as if they belong in an exclusive boutique or smart decorating shop in the old quarter of one of the world's great cities. The plain gold pot looks sophisticated

with the variegated leaves and warm yellow of the nasturtium flowers, and the smudgy violet and gold harlequin patterns are inspired. You can see the violet echoed in soft swathes on the old plaster of the wall, too. The harlequin pattern has been painted freehand. Having experimented with stencils, I find this to be the only way to paint pots.

▲ The soft checkerboard painted on this little container is perfect for the palm potted in golden sand — it appears to be made out of damp and dry sand. Stronger decoration than this would detract from the beautifully planted garden, but light, warm checks give the scene Saint Tropez chic.

Bold delivery

Although chic is restrained, it is never dull. What could be more cheerful on an autumn day than to come upon these chrysanthemums, or an ornamental kale all dressed up for the city in a smart painted pot.

◀Pink, gold, emerald and black are splendid colors with a collar of terra cotta, and it's so easy to do. Paint the container with a coat of black latex or smooth concrete paint and allow to dry. Divide into four segments, then eight (put a dab of pink paint on the pink sections to avoid mistakes), infill with pink. When it is dry, plant.

▲ A touch of cool green paint is all that is required to give further richness to the flowers and foliage of a busy planting of lisianthus.

▶ Painted pots like these shocking pink terra cottas bring extra color and interest to confined spaces, but the main reason for painting pots is to flatter the plants they contain. The solid mass and strong markings of this ornamental kale work well in the bold, plain pot; the double chrysanthemum by its side is perhaps less successful. This fussy plant is too airy to counterbalance such a striking pink shade.

◀The swanlike necks of elegant, white potted phalaenopsis orchids emerge from an artful arrangement of terra cotta pots. Set into a matte black box, they are casually anchored in their mossy base, decorated with lotus seed heads. I can imagine them ending up on a white grand piano, in a white drawing room, at some impossibly fashionable address. Their expensiveness is deceptive — these exquisite creatures last so much longer than ordinary cut flowers.

Pure style

Don't overdeck the garden in garish shades; fashionable pots have one-color planting schemes: black or white flowers for the epitome of chic.

◀ Black flowers are rich and mysterious; a dashing, almost dangerous sight in the garden, they always elicit a comment from guests. I would not be without 'Molly Sanderson' violets: they are so easygoing, performing well in sun and light shade. With regular deadheading and watering, they will reward you with pretty, curious little flowers all summer long, never better than when grown in an old pot.

▶ When you see the first marguerites blossoming in a chic city windowbox, or growing on each side of a front door, you know summer has finally arrived. This whimsical pastry-cook-gothic patterned pot is ideal for these clouds of tiny daisies, light-hearted and elegant as they are. But watch out, marguerites are thirsty plants that need masses of water.

Heavenly host

Soft terra cotta pots cannot be improved upon as a setting for bright spring flowers. This delightful row of early narcissus is effortlessly chic, with an elegant, almost 18th-century charm. Perhaps this is down to the simple flowers and their symmetrical arrangement: plain handmade pots alternating with ones as swagged and bowed as a formal drawing room. To add additional color (by painting the containers, or mixing a selection of plants) would upset the balance — as I'm sure any gardener from the Age of Elegance would agree.

Subtle magic

Two plantings that discreetly take the focus in outdoor living spaces — terra cotta in a supporting role.

◄ The color scheme of this outdoor room is lifted by an elegantly planted pot of heliotrope and scented-leaf geranium. Solanum encloses the walls, its leaf color echoed in a darker shade by the spidery furniture and illuminated by the heliotrope. The pot itself has a patina of lime that harmonizes so well with the brick paving, you barely notice the terra cotta — it becomes a soft smudge, undershadowing the planting.

▶ A large Ali Baba pot has been chosen to give substance to the rare, delicate *Clematis* 'Etoile Rose' with nemesia. How subtly the bell-shaped flowers echo the curves of the container.

Shear control

In the wild, boxwood is fairly unremarkable, but bring it into the garden and what elegance can be yours! This is living architecture that can be controlled and fashioned in wonderful detail.

◀Topiary in washed aubergine- and lemon-cream-colored pots, further dressed with white marble rocks, is effortlessly sophisticated. The color of the containers duplicates the color of the table they dominate. Larger than your average table decoration, they make an impressive sight on plain wood trestles.

▶ This jauntier version is no less controlled. Black-and-white terra cotta nestles in a bed of baby's-tears (soleirolia), planted as ground cover. The effect is a luxurious carpet; miniature boxwood almost merging with the baby's-tears.

▶▶ Too much decoration at the front of the house always looks inappropriate — as indecorous as telling strangers in a bar your life story. Besides, there is not much scope for visual high notes in the private garden, if all the best

tunes have been played out in the street. This front door has achieved the right balance: dignified, interesting, welcoming but not gushing. White paint works well next to the blond stone and the polished-brass door accessories, but what lifts this out of the ordinary is the pair of boxwood spirals in their decorated pots on each side of the step. The pots provide detail and the spirals, beneath the star lantern, add whimsy.

Global poise

Terra cotta is proud of its roots. These are examples from three continents of the world. In each case, the terra cotta has a distinctive ethnic appearance, but also an elegance that transcends its origins. Striking and ornamental, this terra cotta is also surprising.

◀ Europe now, a Tuscan setting: just as in the ancient gardens of Greece and Rome, where terra cotta urns enhanced the symmetry of the garden design, here in a small courtyard planted with lavender, a terra cotta pot is the focal point. The pot is plain yet elegant — it would not be out of place on an urban roof terrace; here, it enhances the earthy tones of the painted house walls.

▲ This crude-looking statue is a Mexican water cooler. Terra cotta has been used for centuries as a primitive cooler for water, olive oil and wine. In a modern capacity, the figure guards the entrance to a sophisticated town house, the blue paint of the wall behind a faint reminder of its origins.

◀ Two groups of old North African amphoras are in perfect balance. They are rustic pots but, removed from their country setting, it is their elegance and simplicity we admire. At the top of this suburban driveway, they are the essence of chic — a bit self-conscious, perhaps, but not incongruous.

On location

Terra cotta forms an integral part of classic designs and simple arrangements, but adds a resonance of its own.

◀ The soft honey color of this stone (like a certain creamy stone of Paris) makes an elegant raised rim for this rectangular pool. (Bricks can be painted in subtle or distressed shades for a similar effect.) Each corner of the pool is studded with an old pot, stony in hue and simply planted with ivy. This creates a feeling of calm. Splashes of color high up could look isolated and disruptive in this setting — better to have the colorful flowers down in the fringe of boxwood, framing the main focus, the pool.

▼ You can almost see the butler complete with silver tray, serving Lapsang Souchong and cucumber sandwiches on this well-bred veranda. Three pots, raised on little feet, become the furniture in an outdoor sitting room. Their position next to the elegant white sofa suggests a lamp and table, and

makes the distant garden more enticing. Any excessive opulence on the part of the agapanthus is calmed down by the casual grouping. However, the chic blue of the painted floor makes you think that if a drop of rain dared to appear at the wrong moment, a pair of white-gloved servants would whisk everything away.

THEATRICAL

With a little imagination and a splash of panache, the world of terra cotta enters a new dimension. In theatrical mode it sets a scene or tells a story. Shamelessly, I have always broken the rules, and where better to do it than your own back yard? If you fancy shocking pink flowerpots, painted in zigzags and planted with red cordylines — why not? Or, you might want a single, striking, show-stopping urn, right in the middle of the garden. Maybe you're an Elvis fan and share The King's penchant for tutti-frutti ice-cream — try a row of matte black pots planted with multicolored flowers. Be inspired! This is terra cotta at its most dramatic.

The new generation of gardeners demands something young and exciting from garden design. While appreciating the beautiful gardens of the past, they (who have never known life without garden stores) want instant gardens and instant style. Designers have had to keep up and, once again, the humble terra cotta pot has awesome potential.

Time to be daring

The opportunities to experiment and have fun are endless: weird and wonderful shapes, painted effects, stencils, outrageous colors, and informal plantings. It is so easy to flatter a plant with a complementary color. Think of gentians (or any blue flower that catches your fancy) in a pot painted azure; marigolds in one of shocking pink or black; pale pink geraniums teamed up with white, gray or silver.

In this chapter I have included terra cotta that both amuses and delights me. The garden is a stage set; terra cotta, the rising star. With effective props and direction, you can achieve drama anywhere.

An inverted amphora, looking like a great dollop of sugared meringue, gives a flourish to the garden and makes an unequivocal focal point wherever you put it. I imagine it surrounded by low boxwood shapes that mimic its curves, placed at the end of a palm-shaded gravel walk, its reflection captured in a circular basin of water. Or, it could be sheltering at the foot of a spectacular *Magnolia grandiflora* next to the house; or standing casually around on its own, up lit, near a swimming pool.

Castaway island

A pool overlooking the sea is one of the greatest luxuries in life — the ideal location, where all you need to do is relax. In this film star's hideaway, you can almost smell the sea, mingling with heady frangipani at the end of a hot day. There's no denying the utopia of this view, but it would not be half as dramatic without the simple pottery bottles and the contained bougainvillea, placed like a Greek chorus, on each side of the proscenium arch.

If terra cotta and flowering plants can improve a panorama like this, think what they can do for an average city roof or yard.

Casablanca

Ingrid Bergman walking into Rick's Bar, "As Time Goes By" softly playing on the piano — to me, these pots are Casablanca, *bringing a touch of Morocco to the garden.*

◀ Just as the audience fell in love with Ingrid Bergman in *Casablanca,* so I fell in love when I first saw these little sago palms. Their elegant fronds and pineapple-shaped centers demand pots of the same spirit — slender and perhaps decorated, as here, with stripes of black and gold: black for a desert night and gold for the sand. The great thing is, this kind of exotic planting is fun in the garden, surrounded with stylish summer flowers. The sago palm (*Cycas revoluta*) is really an oasis plant (prefering moist growing conditions and light shade), but will perform just as successfully in a pot, if you keep it well watered.

▲ This scalloped pot continues the North African theme. It is painted white like a desert building, as if to deflect the heat of the sun, and, with a little imagination, the pierced holes could be tiny, deep windows. Unplanted, positioned on a table, it is a striking focal point, and it could be even more dramatic holding nightlights at a party.

As for planting, a favorite of mine, strappy-leaved black lilyturf (*Ophiopogon*) would look magical in this, winding its way through the holes. Or, try a very young red cordyline, agave or any sort of cactus.

Precious metal

Who would have thought that spraying tall pots silver would look this good? The terra cotta is completely transformed, becoming modern and sleek.

▲ I love these shiny, glittering, crazy pots. It is an old idea, growing herbs on the windowsill, but these silver pots make such a decorative home.

I imagine the pots were sprayed, the green paint added while they were wet, and gravity did the rest. As with the silver pots opposite, the color enhances the planting. Silver and black, to bring out the different pinks, would be another combination to try.

▶ These jars are a natural complement to the thrift they contain. The gray-tone paint flatters the pink flowers and, surprisingly, plants always look good with metallic colors. After all, nature often produces her own: silver-bush (*Convolvulus cneorum*), Matilija poppy (*Romneya coulteri*) and the silvery, willow-leaved pear (*Pyrus salicifolia* 'Pendula') all have decisively metal-colored leaves.

Circus clowns & seaside stripes

Backstage at the theater, wardrobe and makeup departments give terra cotta a leading role to play with artificial flowers and primary stripes.

▶ These wax auricula primroses in their circus-striped pots could not be more theatrical if they tried. Picture them, unashamedly artificial, being dismantled on a Saturday night after the show and wrapped in newspaper. Monday morning, the flowers tweaked, a quick touch-up of paint on the pots, and they will be back on set, exactly where they

were two days previously, in a theater in a different town. Plastic flowers can look tawdry but wax ones are charming, perhaps because the natural material lends quality and richness to the colors.

◄ Striped beach cabanas and umbrellas: these candy-striped pots are full of associations. The subtle blue-gray contrasting with the clearer pinks, yellows and greens reminds me of sun-kissed skin in beachwear. This illusion is helped by the use of an eggshell-colored base and paint on top for the various stripes, suggesting the matte texture of cotton. The stripes glow. Two rows positioned at the foot of these often painted, now peeling gold tiers have all the delightful seediness of a fair on an abandoned pier.

▶ Here, I wanted the stripes on the two terra cotta pots, with their orbs of golden chrysanthemums, to look like the misty horizon of the ocean meeting the sky on a hot day. The blue door, bricks, and general simplicity add to the seaside ambience. Later on, some large shells and surrounding planting of rosemary, lavender and sea holly will enhance the maritime scene.

From Russia with love

Who knows what secrets you could uncover at the Winter Palace? The bare, wintry look of miniature evergreens is a good excuse for an imaginary flight to Russia to indulge in a little malachite.

◀ This pot has the air of a secret agent, failing to disguise itself under a black-purple glaze. It lurks in the garden, conspicuous, yet somehow blending in. There is a touch of genius about its placing, perfectly in harmony with the Scotch thistle (*Onopordum acanthium*), yet at odds with it. The color of the container brings out the matte gray of the thistle's architectural leaves, and its fascinating piecrust lip echoes their serrated edges.

▶ For me, malachite has the romance of Russia, even if only a painted pot on a windowsill. When young, boxwood lollipops are too small for the garden, but set apart they are impressive. I can picture malachite-patterned pots on a balcony, looking terrific planted with boxwood and white petunias.

Can Can!

These gerbera daisies are naughty, with their pretty painted faces. Their gorgeous colors have all the panache of swirling silk skirts at the Moulin Rouge.

▶ A chorus line of pots can give rhythm and excitement to the dreariest windowsill, particularly in the city where every corner must earn its keep. It is not unusual to find the main window of an apartment or townhouse looking out on to nothing more exciting than a lightwell, or worse, an unrelieved brick or concrete wall — you should at least put something nice in the foreground!

This is one of the beauties of terra cotta — you can so easily use it to make a splash of color, when and where it is needed. In this case, I used a line of painted pots to decorate a fountain for a party.

Theatrical

▲ The electric colors of these gerbera daisies demand terra cotta that is quiet, yet sure. A coat of matte black paint seems the obvious choice, as anything bright could upstage the flowers. I always leave the terra cotta rim unpainted for detail.

If you regularly remove the spent flowers, this plant will reward you all summer with a generous display.

Heightening the drama

Certain plants are larger than life, formidable when planted in flamboyant swagged containers.

◀In its pot of masks and swags, this tower of twigs, covered with golden hop, reminds me of an old-fashioned theater box. As the summer goes on, the hop will fill out and become a column of soft-lime-colored leaves; all it asks is a place in the sun. Once established, it is an easygoing pet, which will reward you in the autumn with clusters of double flowers.

A word of caution: the golden hop seeds freely and occasionally a rogue green one appears. Rub these out ruthlessly, or they will take over, leaving you not with gold, but a coarse, green tangle.

▶ This brugmansia is a perfect example of a theatrical plant, from its outrageous, strongly scented trumpet flowers to the lush, tropical leaves. Different, smaller elements in the garden serve to highlight the scale: the ornamentation on the pot, the statue perched on the brick wall, the delicate lavender reined in by a low boxwood hedge, all combining to dramatize this marvelous beast of a tree.

In keeping with their size, brugmansias are greedy feeders and don't like their compost to dry out, especially in hot weather. They will soon tell you if they are thirsty by sulkily drooping their leaves; a good drink and they will perk up, often within the hour. Given a sunny position and adequate food and moisture, these show stoppers are easy to grow, promising a splendid return for very little trouble.

Comic capers

A rubber plant toppling a cone, an echeveria, or could it be a hedgehog?
In cartoon containers, animated plants cause some amusement.

◄◄How futuristic this cone-shaped pot on its impossibly thin legs must have seemed in the early 1950s. A copy made today retains an avant-garde edge. Houseplants like this India rubber tree (*Ficus elastica*), became all the rage after the Second World War. In the light, centrally heated rooms of the new architecture, they were encouraged to grow right up to the ceiling. Today's designers delight in retrospection, traveling back in time to find tongue-in-cheek style.

◄A hedgehog pot holds an echeveria so perfectly, that it could almost be part of the plant. A row of these would look terrific at the base of a sunny glass wall.

▶ An animated planting sits in an equally vibrant, turquoise-glazed container. The gray-blue grass lends height and flourish, its matte leaves a good antidote to the pot's veneer, while the French marigolds and sun roses give substance and color contrast. The terra cotta band around the rim of the pot keeps everything calm.

◀ Planting and styling elevate this terra cotta plant pot to a more dramatic height. It becomes the central focus in this arrangement positioned on an old-fashioned florist's stand. The bright pink of the pot adds flourish to a magnificent orchid; complementary cyclamen and fuchsia flowers provide a subtext; and the malachite urn and striped chair are other glamorous players in this outdoor salon.

Orchids are one of the best-kept secrets of the flower world. As long as they are not overwatered, they will bloom for weeks, sometimes months. In the meantime, you could have bought many other plants: luxurious orchids are excellent value.

Part of the scenery

For many years I worked in the theater. It always fascinated me, as we moved from town to town, how once the set was assembled, the cast felt completely at home — as if we had never moved. It is fun to create the feeling of a stage set at home, a place to escape to at the end of the day, to live out a dream, or to tell a story. When you want to move on to another play or theme, nothing more elaborate than a paintbrush or a garden trowel is required.

▶▶ Imagination and taste have transformed this North African rooftop into a stunning example of theatrical styling. A veritable riot of delicate, ivy-leaved geraniums in a controlled range of clear pinks swamps the seating area, the colors mimicked by the shocking pink tablecloth and deliciously impractical white of the chair covers. The only other color is terra cotta, a ring of pots which links this oasis in the sky to the surrounding cityscape.

In the spotlight

Theatricality relies on immediate effect — once the curtain goes up, the audience's attention must not waver.

▶ Beautifully placed in a spotlight of cobbles, this delicate cordyline takes center-stage as gracefully as Margot Fonteyn. The circular canopy is a clever device, for not only do the individual arches frame the pot, but the overhead protection keeps the scale intimate, doubly enhancing the emphasis of the cordyline in its rippled container. The placing of the canopy is clever, too: it is in front of the house and yet, to reach it, you must take a circuitous route and enter at an oblique angle, through one of the arches.

▶▶ These glowing red walls have instant impact, but it is the generous adobelike terra cotta pots on each side of the gold doors that bring the scene to life. Smaller containers would look prim. One day, the split-leaf philodendron (*Monstera deliciosa*), named for its delicious fruit, will frame the door with overhanging leaves.

▶▶▶ This beautiful jar, with its rope decoration, is a commanding presence. A sea of red lilies, contained by the boxwood hedge, bows like a chorus in deference to the great star, which itself needs no further decoration. I have never come across a pot like this one before. Unusual objects give a garden an extra quality, lifting it out of the ordinary.

Wild & dangerous

◄ A theatrical study in desert textures. Weather-beaten, windswept terra cotta that, when gathered together, conjures up images of the Wild West — from the iron staples of the large repaired piece in the background, to the rare signed amphora. The planting, too, is evocative and masterly: cactus, agave and succulent, beautiful in their variation of shape and texture.

▶ An audacious combination of pot and planting — terra cotta going wild with a faux leopard-skin coat. In its native Mexico, the gray-and-white striped *Agave americana* 'Medio-picta' *alba* produces flowers on spikes up to 25 feet high. Its foliage reminds me of a leopard cub — tempting enough to stroke, but it just might snap at your hand. One *could* remove its sharp teeth, but that seems cruel – far better to pamper it in a decorated container. Borrowed from indoors, a French chair with matching upholstery ceases to be functional. Pot and plant present the ultimate in theatrical styling.

Where to find interesting terra cotta

AW Pottery
2908 Adeline Street
Berkeley, CA 94703
510-549-3901
catalog available

Blue Stone Main
120 Petaluma Boulevard N
Petaluma, CA 94952
707-765-2024

Chelsea Gardens
205 9th Avenue
New York, NY 10011
212-929-2477

Classic Garden Ornaments, Ltd.
Longshadow Gardens
Pomona, IL 62975
618-893-4831
catalog available

The Clay Pot
162 7th Avenue
Brooklyn, NY 11215
718-788-6564

The Grass Roots Garden
131 Spring Street
New York, NY 10012
212-226-2662

International Terra Cotta, Inc.
690 N Robertson Boulevard
Los Angeles, CA 90069
310-657-3752
800-338-9943
catalog available

Jackson's Pottery
6950 Lemmon Avenue
Dallas, TX 75209
214-350-9200

Lexington Gardens
1011 Lexington Ave
New York, NY 10021
212-861-4390

Martin Viette Nursery
PO Box 10
6050 Northern Boulevard
East Norwich, NY 11732
516-922-5530

Merrihew's Sunset Gardens
1526 Ocean Park Boulevard
Santa Monica, CA 90405
310-452-1051

New England Garden Ornaments
PO Box 235
North Brookfield, MA 01535
508-867-4474
catalog available

Orchid Perfection
85 Upper Road
Upper Sandwich, NH 03227
800-497-3891

Pottery Manufacturing and Distributing, Inc.
18881 S Hoover Street
Gardena, CA 90248-4284
800-991-9914

Roger's Gardens
2301 San Joaquin Hills Road
Corona del Mar, CA 92625
714-640-5800

Seibert & Rice
PO Box 365
Short Hills, NJ 07078
973-467-8266
catalog available

Smith & Hawken
various locations nationwide
800-776-3336
catalog available

Stonington Gardens (wholesale)
2682 Coyle Avenue
Elk Grove Village, IL 60007
847-357-9323
catalog available, see:
   Roger's Garden
   Blue Stone Main
   Chelsea Gardens
   Martin Viette Nursery
   Urban Gardens

Sunland Imports
PO Box 3742
Tucson, AZ 85740

Treillage Ltd.
418 East 75th Street
New York, NY 10021
212-535 2288

Urban Gardens
305 Centre Street
Dallas, TX 75208
214-943-6785

Author's acknowledgments

First of all, I would like to thank Kirsty Brackenridge and Sally Cracknell: Kirsty, for her elegant editing and Sally, for her beautiful design. Thanks to Ann Collett, Richard Coates and Mrs Douglas Adams for their friendship and support – in particular Mrs Adams for allowing us to photograph her lovely garden;. Andrew Lawson, the well-known photographer, whose pictures are 'simply the best', in my opinion; Erica Hunningher and Anne Fraser for 'discovering' me, and Frances Lincoln, for her quiet encouragement and lavish hospitality. Lastly, I would like to thank my old friend and colleague, Paul Hollis, one of the nicest, most capable people I have the privilege of knowing.

Publishers' acknowledgments

Frances Lincoln Ltd would like to thank Clifton Nurseries Ltd and Spanish Pots for kindly allowing us to photograph their pots. Thanks also to Sarah Pickering for her design assistance.

Editor   Kirsty Brackenridge
Art Editor   Sally Cracknell
Picture Researcher   Sue Gladstone
Production Controller   Vivien Antwi
Art Director   Caroline Hillier
Editorial Director   Erica Hunningher
Head of Pictures   Anne Fraser

Photographic acknowledgments

a=above b=below l=left r=right c=centre d=designer
Bill Burlington: 2 (d: Alexander Macdonald-Buchanan, The Brooke Pottery) **Neil Campbell-Sharp:** 32–33 & 58l (Westwind, Marlborough, Wiltshire); 67 (d: Lady Puttnam, Kings Mead Mill, Wiltshire) **The Garden Picture Library/ Ron Sutherland:** 114 (d: Nula Caycock & Mathew Bell) **John Glover:** 8–9 (d: Dan Pearson); 34l (d: John Plummer); 62 (Parham Park, Sussex); 85; 86l & r (d: Mark Walker); 92–93; 97r (Langley Boxwood Nursery, Liss, Hampshire); 110 **Georgia Glynn Smith:** 24–25c; 26–27 (Victoria Pots); 54; 55; 66; 86–87c (d: Fiona Lawrenson); 87r; 96 (Blakes Hotel, London); 105 (Victoria Pots); 111; 130; endpapers

Niccolò Grassi: 60l © FLL **Jerry Harpur:** 6–7 (d: Martina Barzi & Josefina Casares, Buenos Aires); 17 (Kiftsgate Court, Gloucestershire); 35r (d: Mel Light, Los Angeles); 71 (d: Robert Broekema, Amsterdam); 80–81c (New York Botanical Garden); 81r (d: Oliver Allen, New York); 100–101 (d: Michael Balston, Devizes, Wiltshire); 119 (Nick & Pam Coote, Oxford); 121 (d: Susan Rowley); 124–125 (Xavier Guerrand Hermés, Marrakech); 129r (d: Penelope Hobhouse) **The Interior Archive/Christopher Simon Sykes:** 60–61c; **Fritz von der Schulenburg** 98l; **Cecilia Innes** 128–129l **Andrea Jones:** 1, 13, 24l & 25r (Licia and Liliana Poggi, Impruneta, Florence); 43 (The Lost Gardens of Heligan, Cornwall); 133 (Licia and Liliana Poggi, Impruneta, Florence) **Michèle Lamontagne:** 75 **Andrew Lawson/ styled by Anthony Noel:** 4–5; 10–11; 14; 47; 72–73; 77; 82–83; 88l; 88–89c (Mrs Adams); 89r; 90r; 97l (Glen Goei); 102–103; 108–109; 112–113; 115; 116–117; 120l; 122; 131 **Andrew Lawson:** 30l & 31r (Powis Castle, Powys); 36 (Cothay Manor, Somerset); 38–39c (Whichford Pottery); 39r (The Old Rectory, Burghfield, Berkshire); 40–41 (Whichford Pottery); 44–45 (The National Trust, Tintinhull House, Somerset); 51r (d: Rupert Golby); 52–53; 56–57 (d: Mirabel Osler); 57r; 58–59r (d: Mirabel Osler); 63; 64–65c (Bourton House, Gloucestershire); 65r (Gothic House, Oxfordshire); 68–69c (Whichford Pottery), 69r (Gothic House, Oxfordshire); 84; 90l; 91 (Bolehyde Manor, Wiltshire); 94 (The Old Rectory, Sudborough, Northamptonshire); 95 (Pamela Schwerdt & Sybille Kreutzberger); 98–99c; 120r (Bourton House, Gloucestershire); 126–127 (Pamela Schwerdt and Sybille Kreutzberger) **Peter Margonelli:** 50–51l (d: Nancy McCabe) **David McDonald:** 70 **Hugh Palmer:** 30–31c (Villa Reale, Florence) **Alex Ramsay:** 48–49; 78 **Vivian Russell:** 18–19; 22 **Ianthe Ruthven:** 28–29r (d: Charles Shoup, Greece) **Derek St. Romaine:** 28l **Erika R. Shank:** 37 (d: Connie Cross, Cutchoge N.Y.); 99r; 101r **Elizabeth Whiting and Associates/Tim Street-Porter:** 106–107 (Giorgio Brignone, Costa Careyes, Mexico) **Steve Wooster:** 20–21 (d: Anthony Noel); 23; 34–35c (Osler Road, Oxford); 68a (Jenny Raworth); 118 (Whichford Pottery)